TO:

_____

FROM:

_____

MESSAGE:

_____

_____

© 2016 Christian Art Gifts, RSA
　　　　Christian Art Gifts Inc., IL, USA

Designed by Christian Art Gifts

Images used under license from Shutterstock.com

Printed in China

ISBN 978-1-4321-1630-9

PROMISES
from GOD
> FOR

MOTHERS

christian
art gifts®

CONTENTS

GOD PROMISES TO BE OUR ...

GOD PROMISES TO ...

CONTENTS

GOD PROMISES GOOD
THINGS WHEN YOU …

GOD PROMISES
TO BE OUR …

COMFORT AND SUPPORT

"Do not be afraid, for I am with you;
I will bless you."

Genesis 26:24 NIV

The LORD will not reject His people; He
will not abandon His special possession.

Psalm 94:14 NLT

He heals the brokenhearted
and binds up their wounds.

Psalm 147:3 NIV

Let Your unfailing love comfort me,
just as You promised me.

Psalm 119:76 NLT

Comfort and Support

"Blessed are those who mourn,
for they will be comforted."

Matthew 5:4 NIV

"I, yes I, am the one who comforts you.
So why are you afraid?"

Isaiah 51:12 NLT

Praise be to the God and Father of
our Lord Jesus Christ, the Father of
compassion and the God of all comfort,
who comforts us in all our troubles.

2 Corinthians 1:3-4 NIV

Though I walk in the midst of trouble,
You preserve my life; You stretch out
Your hand against the wrath of my enemies,
and Your right hand delivers me.

Psalm 138:7 ESV

As the deer longs for streams of water,
so I long for You, O God. I thirst for God,
the living God.

Psalm 42:1-2 NLT

COMFORT AND SUPPORT

The Lord comforts His people and will have
compassion on His afflicted ones.

Isaiah 49:13 NIV

The Lord upholds all who fall, and raises
up all who are bowed down.

Psalm 145:14 NKJV

The Lord is close to the brokenhearted;
He rescues those whose spirits are crushed.

Psalm 34:18 NLT

Weeping may endure for a night,
but joy comes in the morning.

Psalm 30:5 NKJV

"As a mother comforts her child,
so will I comfort you."

Isaiah 66:13 NIV

CUP OF BLESSING

The curse of the Lord is on the house of the wicked, but He blesses the home of the just.

Proverbs 3:33 NKJV

"Blessed are those who hunger and thirst for righteousness, for they shall be satisfied."

Matthew 5:6 ESV

May you be blessed by the Lord, the Maker of heaven and earth.

Psalm 115:15 NIV

Blessed are those whose way is blameless, who walk in the law of the Lord!

Psalm 119:1 ESV

Oh, taste and see that the Lord is good; blessed is the man who trusts in Him!

Psalm 34:8 NKJV

The Lord will indeed give what is good, and our land will yield its harvest.

Psalm 85:12 NIV

CUP OF BLESSING

"Blessed are the pure in heart,
for they shall see God."

Matthew 5:8 NKJV

When You open Your hand, You satisfy the
hunger and thirst of every living thing.
The LORD is righteous in everything
He does; He is filled with kindness.

Psalm 145:16-17 NLT

The blessing of the LORD brings wealth,
without painful toil for it.

Proverbs 10:22 NIV

The LORD bless you and keep you;
the LORD make His face shine upon you,
and be gracious to you; the LORD lift up His
countenance upon you, and give you peace.

Numbers 6:24-26 NKJV

"God blesses those who are merciful,
for they will be shown mercy."

Matthew 5:7 NLT

Cup of Blessing

The LORD is my chosen portion and
my cup; You hold my lot. The lines have
fallen for me in pleasant places; indeed,
I have a beautiful inheritance.

Psalm 16:5-6 ESV

"Blessed are the meek,
for they will inherit the earth."

Matthew 5:5 NIV

All praise to God, the Father of our
Lord Jesus Christ, who has blessed us
with every spiritual blessing in the heavenly
realms because we are united with Christ.

Ephesians 1:3 NLT

The LORD your God will bless you in all
your harvest and in all the work of your
hands, and your joy will be complete.

Deuteronomy 16:15 NIV

Eternal Hope

We have this hope as an anchor
for the soul, firm and secure.

Hebrews 6:19 NIV

Joyful are those whose hope
is in the LORD their God.

Psalm 146:5 NLT

Be strong and take heart,
all you who hope in the LORD.

Psalm 31:24 NIV

Hope in the LORD! For with
the LORD there is steadfast love, and
with Him is plentiful redemption.

Psalm 130:7 ESV

May the God of hope fill you with
all joy and peace as you trust in Him,
so that you may overflow with hope
by the power of the Holy Spirit.

Romans 15:13 NIV

Eternal Hope

Those who hope in the Lord will
renew their strength. They will soar on
wings like eagles; they will run and not
grow weary, they will walk and not be faint.

Isaiah 40:31 NIV

"Know that I am the Lord; those who
hope in Me will not be disappointed."

Isaiah 49:23 NIV

Hope deferred makes the heart sick,
but a dream fulfilled is a tree of life.

Proverbs 13:12 NLT

No one who hopes in You, Lord,
will ever be put to shame.

Psalm 25:3 NIV

The hope of the righteous will be gladness.

Proverbs 10:28 NKJV

Eternal Hope

Rejoice in hope, be patient in tribulation,
be constant in prayer.

Romans 12:12 ESV

Let us hold fast the confession
of our hope without wavering,
for He who promised is faithful.

Hebrews 10:23 ESV

We also glory in our sufferings, because we
know that suffering produces perseverance;
perseverance, character; and character, hope.

Romans 5:3-4 NIV

Through Him we have also obtained access
by faith into this grace in which we stand,
and we rejoice in hope of the glory of God.

Romans 5:2 ESV

Faithful Friend

The LORD's promises are pure, like silver
refined in a furnace, purified seven times over.

Psalm 12:6 NLT

The heavens praise Your wonders,
LORD, Your faithfulness too,
in the assembly of the holy ones.

Psalm 89:5 NIV

The LORD will cover you with His feathers. He
will shelter you with His wings. His faithful
promises are your armor and protection.

Psalm 91:4 NLT

Know therefore that the LORD your
God is God; He is the faithful God,
keeping His covenant of love to a
thousand generations of those who love
Him and keep His commandments.

Deuteronomy 7:9 NIV

The LORD always keeps His promises;
He is gracious in all He does.

Psalm 145:13 NLT

Faithful Friend

If we are faithless, He remains faithful;
He cannot deny Himself.

2 Timothy 2:13 NKJV

Sovereign LORD, You are God!
Your covenant is trustworthy.

2 Samuel 7:28 NIV

Your decrees are very trustworthy;
holiness befits Your house,
O LORD, forevermore.

Psalm 93:5 ESV

God is faithful, who has called
you into fellowship with His Son,
Jesus Christ our Lord.

1 Corinthians 1:9 NIV

Steadfast love will be built up forever; in the
heavens You will establish Your faithfulness.

Psalm 89:2 ESV

Faithful Friend

Your faithfulness extends to
every generation, as enduring
as the earth You created.

Psalm 119:90 NLT

He is the Maker of heaven and earth,
the sea, and everything in them –
He remains faithful forever.

Psalm 146:6 NIV

I will sing of the LORD's unfailing
love forever! Young and old will
hear of Your faithfulness.

Psalm 89:1 NLT

God is not a man, that He should lie,
nor a son of man, that He should repent.
Has He said, and will He not do? Or has
He spoken, and will He not make it good?

Numbers 23:19 NKJV

Fountain of Joy

The joy of the LORD is your strength.
Nehemiah 8:10 NKJV

Glory in His holy name; let the hearts
of those who seek the LORD rejoice.
Psalm 105:3 NIV

This is the day that the LORD has made;
let us rejoice and be glad in it.
Psalm 118:24 ESV

Those who sow with tears will
reap with songs of joy.
Psalm 126:5 NIV

"Rejoice because your names
are written in heaven."
Luke 10:20 NKJV

Fountain of Joy

"Be happy! Yes, leap for joy!
For a great reward awaits you in heaven."

Luke 6:23 NLT

Honor and majesty are before Him;
strength and gladness are in His place.

1 Chronicles 16:27 NKJV

When Your words came, I ate them;
they were my joy and my heart's delight.

Jeremiah 15:16 NIV

Let all those who seek You rejoice and be
glad in You; and let those who love
Your salvation say continually,
"Let God be magnified!"

Psalm 70:4 NKJV

You turned my wailing into dancing;
You removed my sackcloth
and clothed me with joy.

Psalm 30:11 NIV

Fountain of Joy

Those who look to Him for help
will be radiant with joy; no shadow
of shame will darken their faces.

Psalm 34:5 NLT

The precepts of the LORD are right, giving
joy to the heart. The commands of the LORD
are radiant, giving light to the eyes.

Psalm 19:8 NIV

Light shines on the godly, and joy
on those whose hearts are right.

Psalm 97:11 NLT

The LORD has done great things for us,
and we are filled with joy.

Psalm 126:3 NIV

Shouts of joy and victory resound in
the tents of the righteous: "The LORD's
right hand has done mighty things!"

Psalm 118:15 NIV

GUIDE FOR LIFE

The LORD will guide you always; He will
satisfy your needs in a sun-scorched land
and will strengthen your frame. You will
be like a well-watered garden, like a
spring whose waters never fail.

Isaiah 58:11 NIV

Jesus said to him, "I am the way,
the truth, and the life. No one comes
to the Father except through Me."

John 14:6 NKJV

Show me Your ways, LORD, teach me
Your paths. Guide me in Your truth and
teach me, for You are God my Savior,
and my hope is in You all day long.

Psalm 25:4-5 NIV

Send out Your light and Your truth; let
them guide me. Let them lead me to Your
holy mountain, to the place where You live.

Psalm 43:3 NLT

GUIDE FOR LIFE

Teach me to do Your will, for You are my God!
Let Your good Spirit lead me on level ground!
Psalm 143:10 ESV

Your word is a lamp to guide
my feet and a light for my path.
Psalm 119:105 NLT

May the Lord direct your hearts into
God's love and Christ's perseverance.
2 Thessalonians 3:5 NIV

The LORD directs the steps of the godly.
He delights in every detail of their lives.
Though they stumble, they will never fall,
for the LORD holds them by the hand.
Psalm 37:23-24 NLT

Whether you turn to the right or to the left,
your ears will hear a voice behind you,
saying, "This is the way; walk in it."
Isaiah 30:21 NIV

Guide for Life

Direct my steps by Your word, and
let no iniquity have dominion over me.

Psalm 119:133 NKJV

All who are led by the Spirit of
God are children of God.

Romans 8:14 NLT

"I will go before you and make the crooked
places straight; I will break in pieces the
gates of bronze and cut the bars of iron."

Isaiah 45:2 NKJV

God is our God for ever and ever;
He will be our guide even to the end.

Psalm 48:14 NIV

For the word of the LORD is upright,
and all His work is done in faithfulness.

Psalm 33:4 ESV

May He give you the desire of your
heart and make all your plans succeed.

Psalm 20:4 NIV

Omnipresent God

God has said, "Never will I leave you;
never will I forsake you."

Hebrews 13:5 NIV

I can never escape from Your Spirit! I can
never get away from Your presence! If I go
up to heaven, You are there; if I go down to
the grave, You are there. If I ride the wings of
the morning, if I dwell by the farthest oceans,
even there Your hand will guide me, and
Your strength will support me.

Psalm 139:7-10 NLT

The eyes of the LORD are in every place,
keeping watch on the evil and the good.

Proverbs 15:3 NKJV

His purpose was for the nations to seek after
God and perhaps feel their way toward Him
and find Him – though He is not far from
any one of us. For in Him we live and move
and exist. As some of your own poets
have said, "We are His offspring."

Acts 17:27-28 NLT

Omnipresent God

The Son is the image of the invisible God,
the firstborn over all creation. For in Him
all things were created: things in heaven
and on earth, visible and invisible, whether
thrones or powers or rulers or authorities;
all things have been created through Him
and for Him. He is before all things,
and in Him all things hold together.

Colossians 1:15-17 NIV

The LORD says: "Heaven is My throne,
and the earth is My footstool. Could
you build Me a temple as good as that?
Could you build Me such a resting place?"

Isaiah 66:1 NLT

For thus says the One who is high and lifted
up, who inhabits eternity, whose name is
Holy: "I dwell in the high and holy place,
and also with him who is of a contrite and
lowly spirit, to revive the spirit of the lowly,
and to revive the heart of the contrite."

Isaiah 57:15 ESV

Omnipresent God

Before the mountains were born or You
brought forth the whole world, from
everlasting to everlasting You are God.

Psalm 90:2 NIV

Look, I go forward, but He is not there,
and backward, but I cannot perceive Him;
when He works on the left hand, I cannot
behold Him; when He turns to the right
hand, I cannot see Him. But He knows the
way that I take; when He has tested me,
I shall come forth as gold.

Job 23:8-10 NKJV

I have set the LORD always before me;
because He is at my right hand,
I shall not be shaken.

Psalm 16:8 ESV

The LORD will stay with you as long as
you stay with Him! Whenever you
seek Him, you will find Him.

2 Chronicles 15:2 NLT

Path to Peace

"I am leaving you with a gift – peace of
mind and heart. And the peace I give
is a gift the world cannot give.
So don't be troubled or afraid."

John 14:27 NLT

The mind governed by the
Spirit is life and peace.

Romans 8:6 NIV

Jesus said, "Come to Me, all of you
who are weary and carry heavy
burdens, and I will give you rest."

Matthew 11:28 NLT

When a man's ways please
the LORD, He makes even his
enemies to be at peace with him.

Proverbs 16:7 NKJV

Great peace have those who love Your law,
and nothing can make them stumble.

Psalm 119:165 NIV

PATH TO PEACE

The peace of God, which surpasses
all understanding, will guard your
hearts and your minds in Christ Jesus.

Philippians 4:7 ESV

Let the peace of Christ rule in your hearts.

Colossians 3:15 ESV

You will keep in perfect peace those
whose minds are steadfast,
because they trust in You.

Isaiah 26:3 NIV

I will both lie down in peace, and sleep; for
You alone, O LORD, make me dwell in safety.

Psalm 4:8 NKJV

"Glory to God in the highest heaven,
and on earth peace to those on
whom His favor rests."

Luke 2:14 NIV

PATH TO PEACE

Because of God's tender mercy,
the morning light from heaven is
about to break upon us, to guide
us to the path of peace.
Luke 1:78-79 NLT

The kingdom of God is not a matter
of eating and drinking but of righteousness
and peace and joy in the Holy Spirit.
Romans 14:17 ESV

Submit to God and be at peace with Him;
in this way prosperity will come to you.
Job 22:21 NIV

God is not a God of confusion but of peace.
1 Corinthians 14:33 ESV

The God of peace be with you.
Romans 15:33 NIV

SAVING GRACE

God gives us grace and glory.
The LORD will withhold no good thing
from those who do what is right.

Psalm 84:11 NLT

With minds that are alert and fully sober, set
your hope on the grace to be brought to you
when Jesus Christ is revealed at His coming.

1 Peter 1:13 NIV

To each one of us grace has been
given as Christ apportioned it.

Ephesians 4:7 NIV

"My grace is sufficient for you, for
My power is made perfect in weakness."

2 Corinthians 12:9 ESV

God saved you by His grace when
you believed. And you can't take
credit for this; it is a gift from God.

Ephesians 2:8 NLT

Saving Grace

God is able to make all grace abound to you,
so that having all sufficiency in all things at all
times, you may abound in every good work.

2 Corinthians 9:8 ESV

Sin is no longer your master, for you
no longer live under the requirements
of the law. Instead, you live under the
freedom of God's grace.

Romans 6:14 NLT

Let us then approach God's throne
of grace with confidence, so that we
may receive mercy and find grace to
help us in our time of need.

Hebrews 4:16 NIV

From His abundance we have all received
one gracious blessing after another.

John 1:16 NLT

SAVING GRACE

In Him we have redemption through
His blood, the forgiveness of sins,
according to the riches of His grace.

Ephesians 1:7 NKJV

We are all saved the same way, by the
undeserved grace of the Lord Jesus.

Acts 15:11 NLT

You know the generous grace of our
Lord Jesus Christ. Though He was rich,
yet for your sakes He became poor, so that
by His poverty He could make you rich.

2 Corinthians 8:9 NLT

Because of His grace He declared
us righteous and gave us confidence
that we will inherit eternal life.

Titus 3:7 NLT

SHIELD OF PROTECTION

The LORD keeps you from all harm and watches over your life. The LORD keeps watch over you as you come and go, both now and forever.

Psalm 121:7-8 NLT

The name of the LORD is a fortified tower; the righteous run to it and are safe.

Proverbs 18:10 NIV

The LORD is my fortress, protecting me from danger, so why should I tremble?

Psalm 27:1 NLT

The Lord is faithful, and He will strengthen you and protect you from the evil one.

2 Thessalonians 3:3 NIV

I will say of the Lord, "He is my refuge and my fortress; my God, in Him I will trust."

Psalm 91:2 NKJV

SHIELD OF PROTECTION

The LORD your God will personally
go ahead of you. He will neither fail
you nor abandon you.

Deuteronomy 31:6 NLT

"I am the LORD your God who takes
hold of your right hand and says to you,
Do not fear; I will help you."

Isaiah 41:13 NIV

With every bone in my body I will praise
Him: "LORD, who can compare with You?
Who else rescues the helpless from
the strong? Who else protects the helpless
and poor from those who rob them?"

Psalm 35:10 NLT

"Fear not, for I am with you; be not dismayed,
for I am your God; I will strengthen you,
I will help you, I will uphold you."

Isaiah 41:10 ESV

Shield of Protection

Even when I walk through the darkest
valley, I will not be afraid, for You,
Lord, are close beside me. Your rod and
Your staff protect and comfort me.

Psalm 23:4 NLT

As for me, it is good to be near God.
I have made the Sovereign Lord my refuge;
I will tell of all Your deeds.

Psalm 73:28 NIV

The Lord is on my side; I will not fear.
What can man do to me?

Psalm 118:6 ESV

The Lord protects all those who love Him,
but He destroys the wicked.

Psalm 145:20 NLT

The Lord protects the unwary;
when I was brought low, He saved me.

Psalm 116:6 NIV

Source of Confidence

Blessed are those who trust in
the Lord and have made the Lord
their hope and confidence.

Jeremiah 17:7 NLT

In the fear of the Lord there is
strong confidence, and His children
will have a place of refuge.

Proverbs 14:26 NKJV

We have placed our confidence in Him,
and He will continue to rescue us.

2 Corinthians 1:10 NLT

It is better to trust in the Lord
than to put confidence in man.

Psalm 118:8 NKJV

We can say with confidence, "The Lord
is my helper, so I will have no fear."

Hebrews 13:6 NLT

Source of Confidence

Such is the confidence that we have through Christ toward God. Not that we are sufficient in ourselves to claim anything as coming from us, but our sufficiency is from God.

2 Corinthians 3:4-5 ESV

You have been my hope, Sovereign Lord, my confidence since my youth.

Psalm 71:5 NIV

By awesome deeds in righteousness You will answer us, O God of our salvation, You who are the confidence of all the ends of the earth, and of the far-off seas.

Psalm 65:5 NKJV

The Lord will be your confidence and will keep your foot from being caught.

Proverbs 3:26 NIV

Now this is the confidence that we have in Him, that if we ask anything according to His will, He hears us.

1 John 5:14 NKJV

Source of Confidence

The fruit of that righteousness will
be peace; its effect will be quietness
and confidence forever.

Isaiah 32:17 NIV

Let us who live in the light be clearheaded,
protected by the armor of faith and
love, and wearing as our helmet
the confidence of our salvation.

1 Thessalonians 5:8 NLT

The law never made anything perfect.
But now we have confidence in a better
hope, through which we draw near to God.

Hebrews 7:19 NLT

Because of Christ and our faith in Him,
we can now come boldly and
confidently into God's presence.

Ephesians 3:12 NLT

Voice of Encouragement

"Be strong and courageous! Do not
be afraid or discouraged. For the Lord
your God is with you wherever you go."

Joshua 1:9 NLT

You, Lord, hear the desire of the
afflicted; You encourage them, and
You listen to their cry, defending the
fatherless and the oppressed.

Psalm 10:17-18 NIV

The Scriptures give us hope and
encouragement as we wait patiently
for God's promises to be fulfilled.
May God, who gives this patience
and encouragement, help you live in
complete harmony with each other.

Romans 15:4-5 NLT

God has not given us a spirit of fear, but of
power and of love and of a sound mind.

2 Timothy 1:7 NKJV

Voice of Encouragement

Worry weighs a person down;
an encouraging word cheers a person up.

Proverbs 12:25 NLT

On the day I called, You answered me;
my strength of soul You increased.

Psalm 138:3 ESV

May our Lord Jesus Christ Himself and God
our Father, who loved us and by His grace
gave us eternal encouragement and good
hope, encourage your hearts and strengthen
you in every good deed and word.

2 Thessalonians 2:16-17 NIV

The humble will see their God at work
and be glad. Let all who seek God's help
be encouraged. For the LORD hears the
cries of the needy.

Psalm 69:32-33 NLT

Voice of Encouragement

Encourage one another and build each
other up, just as in fact you are doing.

1 Thessalonians 5:11 NIV

Your words have supported those
who were falling; you encouraged
those with shaky knees.

Job 4:4 NLT

Because God wanted to make the
unchanging nature of His purpose very
clear to the heirs of what was promised, He
confirmed it with an oath. God did this so
that, by two unchangeable things in which
it is impossible for God to lie, we who have
fled to take hold of the hope set before us
may be greatly encouraged.

Hebrews 6:17-18 NIV

Be strong and courageous;
do not be afraid or lose heart!

1 Chronicles 22:13 NLT

GOD

PROMISES TO ...

ANSWER OUR PRAYERS

If we know that He hears us in whatever we ask, we know that we have the requests that we have asked of Him.

1 John 5:15 ESV

"If My people will humble themselves, and pray and seek My face, and turn from their wicked ways, then I will hear from heaven, and will forgive their sin and heal their land."

2 Chronicles 7:14 NKJV

We will receive from Him whatever we ask because we obey Him and do the things that please Him.

1 John 3:22 NLT

ANSWER OUR PRAYERS

They cried to the Lord in their trouble, and
He delivered them from their distress.

Psalm 107:28 ESV

In my distress I called upon the Lord,
and cried out to my God; He heard my
voice from His temple, and my cry
came before Him, even to His ears.

Psalm 18:6 NKJV

"If you remain in Me and My
words remain in you, ask whatever
you wish, and it will be done for you."

John 15:7 NIV

"I tell you the truth, you can say to this
mountain, 'May you be lifted up and thrown
into the sea,' and it will happen. But you
must really believe it will happen and have
no doubt in your heart. I tell you, you can
pray for anything, and if you believe that
you've received it, it will be yours."

Mark 11:23-24 NLT

Answer Our Prayers

"When they call on Me, I will answer;
I will be with them in trouble. I will
rescue and honor them."

Psalm 91:15 NLT

"Whatever you ask of the Father in My
name, He will give it to you. "

John 16:23 ESV

"Call to Me and I will answer you
and tell you great and unsearchable
things you do not know."

Jeremiah 33:3 NIV

"If two of you agree here on earth
concerning anything you ask, My Father
in heaven will do it for you."

Matthew 18:19 NLT

The eyes of the Lord are on the righteous
and His ears are attentive to their prayer.

1 Peter 3:12 NIV

Care for His Children

Cast your cares on the Lord and
He will sustain you; He will never
let the righteous be shaken.

Psalm 55:22 NIV

He will not let your foot be moved;
He who keeps you will not slumber.

Psalm 121:3 ESV

What is man that You are mindful of
him, and the son of man that You visit
him? For You have made him a little
lower than the angels, and You have
crowned him with glory and honor.

Psalm 8:4-5 NKJV

The Lord keeps watch over you as you
come and go, both now and forever.

Psalm 121:8 NLT

The Lord has been mindful of us;
He will bless us. He will bless those who
fear the Lord, both small and great.

Psalm 115:12-13 NKJV

Care for His Children

I will be glad and rejoice in Your unfailing love, for You have seen my troubles, and You care about the anguish of my soul.

Psalm 31:7 NLT

Cast all your anxiety on Him because He cares for you.

1 Peter 5:7 NIV

"I will be your God throughout your lifetime – until your hair is white with age. I made you and I will care for you. I will carry you along and save you."

Isaiah 46:4 NLT

When I thought, "My foot slips," Your steadfast love, O LORD, held me up. When the cares of my heart are many, Your consolations cheer my soul.

Psalm 94:18-19 ESV

CARE FOR HIS CHILDREN

"Are not two sparrows sold for a copper
coin? And not one of them falls to the
ground apart from your Father's will.
The very hairs of your head are all
numbered. Do not fear therefore; you
are of more value than many sparrows."

Matthew 10:29-31 NKJV

You go before me and follow me. You place
Your hand of blessing on my head.
Such knowledge is too wonderful for me,
too great for me to understand!

Psalm 139:5-6 NLT

"Can a woman forget her nursing child,
that she should have no compassion on the
son of her womb? Even these may forget,
yet I will not forget you."

Isaiah 49:15 ESV

"If God cares so wonderfully for wildflowers
that are here today and thrown into the fire
tomorrow, He will certainly care for you."

Matthew 6:30 NLT

Forgive All Our Sins

If we confess our sins to Him, He is
faithful and just to forgive us our sins
and to cleanse us from all wickedness.

1 John 1:9 NLT

As far as the east is from the west, so far has
He removed our transgressions from us.

Psalm 103:12 NIV

"Though your sins are like scarlet, they
shall be as white as snow; though they are
red as crimson, they shall be like wool."

Isaiah 1:18 NIV

Now there is no condemnation for those
who belong to Christ Jesus. And because
you belong to Him, the power of the life-
giving Spirit has freed you from the
power of sin that leads to death.

Romans 8:1-2 NLT

Forgive All Our Sins

If anyone sins, we have an Advocate
with the Father, Jesus Christ the righteous.
And He Himself is the propitiation for
our sins, and not for ours only but
also for the whole world.

1 John 2:1-2 NKJV

Who is a God like You, who pardons sin and
forgives the transgression of the remnant
of His inheritance? You do not stay angry
forever but delight to show mercy. You
will again have compassion on us; You
will tread our sins underfoot and hurl all
our iniquities into the depths of the sea.

Micah 7:18-19 NIV

Christ was offered once for all time as a
sacrifice to take away the sins of many
people. He will come again, not to deal
with our sins, but to bring salvation to
all who are eagerly waiting for Him.

Hebrews 9:28 NLT

Forgive All Our Sins

You are a forgiving God, gracious
and compassionate, slow to anger
and abounding in love.

Nehemiah 9:17 NIV

God freely and graciously declares that we
are righteous. He did this through Christ
Jesus when He freed us from the penalty
for our sins. For God presented Jesus as the
sacrifice for sin. People are made right with
God when they believe that Jesus sacrificed
His life, shedding His blood.

Romans 3:24-25 NLT

It is the power of God that brings
salvation to everyone who believes.

Romans 1:16 NIV

You were dead because of your sins and
because your sinful nature was not yet cut
away. Then God made you alive with Christ,
for He forgave all our sins. He canceled the
record of the charges against us and took it
away by nailing it to the cross.

Colossians 2:13-14 NLT

Help in Times of Trial

Blessed is the one who perseveres under trial
because, having stood the test, that person
will receive the crown of life.

James 1:12 NIV

I consider that the sufferings of this present
time are not worth comparing with the glory
that is to be revealed to us.

Romans 8:18 ESV

Consider it pure joy, my brothers and sisters,
whenever you face trials of many kinds,
because you know that the testing of your
faith develops perseverance. Let perseverance
finish its work so that you may be mature and
complete, not lacking anything.

James 1:2-4 NIV

The God of all grace, who called you to
His eternal glory in Christ, after you have
suffered a little while, will Himself restore
you and make you strong, firm and steadfast.

1 Peter 5:10 NIV

Help in Times of Trial

Since He Himself has gone through suffering and testing, He is able to help us when we are being tested.

Hebrews 2:18 NLT

If you suffer for doing good and you endure it, this is commendable before God.

1 Peter 2:20 NIV

Those who suffer according to God's will should commit themselves to their faithful Creator and continue to do good.

1 Peter 4:19 NIV

"When you go through deep waters, I will be with you. When you go through rivers of difficulty, you will not drown. When you walk through the fire of oppression, you will not be burned up; the flames will not consume you."

Isaiah 43:2 NLT

Help in Times of Trial

I love the LORD because He hears my
voice and my prayer for mercy. Because
He bends down to listen, I will pray
as long as I have breath!

Psalm 116:1-2 NLT

Be strong and do not give up,
for your work will be rewarded.

2 Chronicles 15:7 NIV

The Lord knows how to rescue godly
people from their trials.

2 Peter 2:9 NLT

Let us throw off everything that hinders and
the sin that so easily entangles. And let us run
with perseverance the race marked out for us.

Hebrews 12:1 NIV

Love Unconditionally

"As the Father loved Me, I also have loved you; abide in My love. If you keep My commandments, you will abide in My love, just as I have kept My Father's commandments and abide in His love."

John 15:9-10 NKJV

I am convinced that neither death nor life, neither angels nor demons, neither the present nor the future, nor any powers, neither height nor depth, nor anything else in all creation, will be able to separate us from the love of God that is in Christ Jesus our Lord.

Romans 8:38-39 NIV

We are more than conquerors through Him who loved us.

Romans 8:37 ESV

"I have loved you with an everlasting love; I have drawn you with unfailing kindness."

Jeremiah 31:3 NIV

Love Unconditionally

"I lavish unfailing love for a thousand
generations on those who love Me
and obey My commands."

Deuteronomy 5:10 NLT

This is love: not that we loved God,
but that He loved us and sent His
Son as an atoning sacrifice for our sins.

1 John 4:10 NIV

"For God so loved the world that
He gave His only begotten Son, that
whoever believes in Him should not
perish but have everlasting life."

John 3:16 NKJV

Give thanks to the LORD, for He is good;
His love endures forever.

Psalm 106:1 NIV

"A new commandment I give to you,
that you love one another: just as I have
loved you, you also are to love one another."

John 13:34 ESV

Love Unconditionally

God's love has been poured out into
our hearts through the Holy Spirit,
who has been given to us.

Romans 5:5 NIV

Your steadfast love, O Lord, extends to the
heavens, Your faithfulness to the clouds.
Your righteousness is like the mountains
of God; Your judgments are like the great
deep; man and beast You save, O Lord.
How precious is Your steadfast love, O God!
The children of mankind take refuge in the
shadow of Your wings.

Psalm 36:5-7 ESV

May you experience the love
of Christ, though it is too great to
understand fully. Then you will be made
complete with all the fullness of life and
power that comes from God.

Ephesians 3:19 NLT

I trust in Your unfailing love;
my heart rejoices in Your salvation.

Psalm 13:5 NIV

MAKE WISE THE SIMPLE

The law of the LORD is perfect, refreshing
the soul. The statutes of the LORD are
trustworthy, making wise the simple.

Psalm 19:7 NIV

If you need wisdom, ask our generous God,
and He will give it to you. He will not
rebuke you for asking.

James 1:5 NLT

"I will instruct you and teach you in
the way you should go; I will counsel
you with My loving eye on you."

Psalm 32:8 NIV

The entrance of Your words gives light;
it gives understanding to the simple.

Psalm 119:130 NKJV

The LORD gives wisdom; from His mouth
come knowledge and understanding.

Proverbs 2:6 NIV

MAKE WISE THE SIMPLE

God gives wisdom, knowledge,
and joy to those who please Him.

Ecclesiastes 2:26 NLT

To God belong wisdom and power;
counsel and understanding are His.

Job 12:13 NIV

Do not forsake wisdom, and she will protect
you; love her, and she will watch over you.

Proverbs 4:6 NIV

Fear of the LORD is the foundation
of true wisdom. All who obey His
commandments will grow in wisdom.

Psalm 111:10 NLT

The wisdom that comes from heaven is first
of all pure; then peace-loving, considerate,
submissive, full of mercy and good fruit,
impartial and sincere.

James 3:17 NIV

Make Wise the Simple

Wisdom is sweet to your soul. If you find it, you will have a bright future, and your hopes will not be cut short.

Proverbs 24:14 NLT

By wisdom a house is built, and by understanding it is established; by knowledge the rooms are filled with all precious and pleasant riches.

Proverbs 24:3-4 ESV

The fear of the LORD is the beginning of wisdom, and knowledge of the Holy One is understanding.

Proverbs 9:10 NIV

Wisdom will enter your heart, and knowledge will fill you with joy. Wise choices will watch over you. Understanding will keep you safe. Wisdom will save you from evil people, from those whose words are twisted.

Proverbs 2:10-12 NLT

Provide All You Need

"Your Father knows what you
need before you ask Him."

Matthew 6:8 NIV

God shall supply all your need according
to His riches in glory by Christ Jesus.

Philippians 4:19 NKJV

"Give, and it will be given to you.
A good measure, pressed down, shaken
together and running over, will be poured
into your lap. For with the measure you
use, it will be measured to you."

Luke 6:38 NIV

"Therefore do not be anxious, saying, 'What
shall we eat?' or 'What shall we drink?' or
'What shall we wear?' For the Gentiles seek
after all these things, and your heavenly
Father knows that you need them all."

Matthew 6:31-32 ESV

PROVIDE ALL YOU NEED

"Consider the ravens, for they neither sow nor reap, which have neither storehouse nor barn; and God feeds them. Of how much more value are you than the birds?"

Luke 12:24 NKJV

"I will open the windows of heaven for you. I will pour out a blessing so great you won't have enough room to take it in. Try it! Put Me to the test!"

Malachi 3:10 NLT

He will give the rain for your land in its season, the early rain and the later rain, that you may gather in your grain and your wine and your oil. And He will give grass in your fields for your livestock, and you shall eat and be full.

Deuteronomy 11:14-15 ESV

The LORD is my shepherd;
I have all that I need.

Psalm 23:1 NLT

Provide All You Need

He who supplies seed to the sower and
bread for food will also supply and increase
your store of seed and will enlarge the
harvest of your righteousness.

2 Corinthians 9:10 NIV

"Every moving thing that lives
shall be food for you. I have given you
all things, even as the green herbs."

Genesis 9:3 NKJV

You care for the land and water it; You
enrich it abundantly. The streams of God
are filled with water to provide the people
with grain, for so You have ordained it.

Psalm 65:9 NIV

His divine power has given us everything
we need for a godly life through our
knowledge of Him who called us by
His own glory and goodness.

2 Peter 1:3 NIV

Strengthen the Weak

The Lord gives His people strength.
The Lord blesses them with peace.

Psalm 29:11 NLT

God is our refuge and strength,
an ever-present help in trouble.

Psalm 46:1 NIV

The Sovereign Lord is my strength!
He makes me as surefooted as a deer,
able to tread upon the heights.

Habakkuk 3:19 NLT

The Lord is my strength and my shield;
in Him my heart trusts, and I am helped;
my heart exults, and with my song
I give thanks to Him.

Psalm 28:7 ESV

In Your strength I can crush an army;
with my God I can scale any wall.

Psalm 18:29 NLT

Strengthen the Weak

Be strong in the Lord and in
His mighty power.

Ephesians 6:10 NIV

The LORD is my strength and my song;
He has given me victory. This is my God,
and I will praise Him – my father's God,
and I will exalt Him!

Exodus 15:2 NLT

"In repentance and rest is your salvation,
in quietness and trust is your strength."

Isaiah 30:15 NIV

Turn to God. Then times of refreshment
will come from the presence of the Lord.

Acts 3:19-20 NLT

"I will seek the lost, and I will bring back
the strayed, and I will bind up the injured,
and I will strengthen the weak."

Ezekiel 34:16 ESV

Strengthen the Weak

The LORD is my strength and my song;
He has given me victory.

Psalm 118:14 NLT

God is my strength and power,
and He makes my way perfect.
He makes my feet like the feet of deer,
and sets me on my high places.

2 Samuel 22:33-34 NKJV

I thank and praise You, God of my ancestors,
for You have given me wisdom and strength.

Daniel 2:23 NLT

He gives strength to the weary and
increases the power of the weak.

Isaiah 40:29 NIV

My health may fail, and my spirit may
grow weak, but God remains the strength
of my heart; He is mine forever.

Psalm 73:26 NLT

GOD PROMISES GOOD THINGS WHEN YOU …

DISCIPLINE YOUR CHILDREN

Direct your children onto
the right path, and when they
are older, they will not leave it.

Proverbs 22:6 NLT

"All your children will be taught by the
LORD, and great will be their peace. In
righteousness you will be established."

Isaiah 54:13-14 NIV

Do not provoke your children to anger
by the way you treat them. Rather,
bring them up with the discipline and
instruction that comes from the Lord.

Ephesians 6:4 NLT

Discipline Your Children

Do not provoke your children,
lest they become discouraged.

Colossians 3:21 ESV

No discipline is enjoyable while it is
happening – it's painful! But afterward
there will be a peaceful harvest of right
living for those who are trained in this way.

Hebrews 12:11 NLT

Whoever spares the rod hates their children,
but the one who loves their children is
careful to discipline them.

Proverbs 13:24 NIV

To discipline a child produces wisdom,
but a mother is disgraced by an
undisciplined child.

Proverbs 29:15 NLT

Foolishness is bound up in the
heart of a child; the rod of correction
will drive it far from him.

Proverbs 22:15 NKJV

Discipline Your Children

Children, obey your parents in everything,
for this pleases the Lord.

Colossians 3:20 ESV

The righteous lead blameless lives;
blessed are their children after them.

Proverbs 20:7 NIV

"Honor your father and your mother,
that your days may be long in the land
that the LORD your God is giving you."

Exodus 20:12 ESV

Children's children are a crown to the aged,
and parents are the pride of their children.

Proverbs 17:16 NIV

Discipline your children, and they will
give you peace of mind and will make
your heart glad. When people do not
accept divine guidance, they run wild.
But whoever obeys the law is joyful.

Proverbs 29:17-18 ESV

DISPLAY A HEART OF THANKSGIVING

Give thanks to the LORD and proclaim
His greatness. Let the whole world
know what He has done.

Psalm 105:1 NLT

Thanks be to God, who in Christ always
leads us in triumphal procession, and
through us spreads the fragrance of the
knowledge of Him everywhere.

2 Corinthians 2:14 ESV

It is good to give thanks to the LORD, to
sing praises to the Most High. It is good to
proclaim Your unfailing love in the morning,
Your faithfulness in the evening.

Psalm 92:1-2 NLT

Come, let us sing for joy to the LORD;
let us shout aloud to the Rock of our
salvation. Let us come before Him with
thanksgiving and extol Him with music
and song. For the LORD is the great God,
the great King above all gods.

Psalm 95:1-3 NIV

Display a Heart of Thanksgiving

You made all the delicate, inner parts
of my body and knit me together in my
mother's womb. Thank You for making me
so wonderfully complex! Your workmanship
is marvelous – how well I know it.

Psalm 139:13-14 NLT

Enter His gates with thanksgiving and
His courts with praise; give thanks to
Him and praise His name.

Psalm 100:4 NIV

We give thanks to You, O God, we give
thanks! For Your wondrous works
declare that Your name is near.

Psalm 75:1 NKJV

I will give thanks to the LORD with my whole
heart; I will recount all of Your wonderful
deeds. I will be glad and exult in You; I will
sing praise to Your name, O Most High.

Psalm 9:1-2 NLT

Display a Heart of Thanksgiving

Sing and make music from your heart to
the Lord, always giving thanks to God
the Father for everything, in the
name of our Lord Jesus Christ.

Ephesians 5:19-20 NIV

Be thankful in all circumstances,
for this is God's will for you who
belong to Christ Jesus.

1 Thessalonians 5:18 NLT

"The one who offers thanksgiving
as his sacrifice glorifies Me; to one who
orders his way rightly I will show the
salvation of God!"

Psalm 50:23 ESV

Make thankfulness your sacrifice to God, and
keep the vows you made to the Most High.

Psalm 50:14 NLT

Humble Yourself

Humble yourselves in the sight
of the Lord, and He will lift you up.

James 4:10 NKJV

True humility and fear of the LORD
lead to riches, honor, and long life.

Proverbs 22:4 NLT

Clothe yourselves, all of you, with humility
toward one another, for "God opposes
the proud but gives grace to the humble."
Humble yourselves, therefore, under the
mighty hand of God so that at the proper
time He may exalt you.

1 Peter 5:5-6 ESV

"I will bless those who have humble and
contrite hearts, who tremble at My word."

Isaiah 66:2 NLT

HUMBLE YOURSELF

"Truly, I say to you, unless you turn and become like children, you will never enter the kingdom of heaven. Whoever humbles himself like this child is the greatest in the kingdom of heaven."

Matthew 18:3-4 ESV

Pride leads to disgrace, but with humility comes wisdom.

Proverbs 11:2 NLT

He has shown you, O mortal, what is good. And what does the LORD require of you? To act justly and to love mercy and to walk humbly with your God.

Micah 6:8 NIV

A man's pride will bring him low, but the humble in spirit will retain honor.

Proverbs 29:23 NKJV

The LORD supports the humble, but He brings the wicked down into the dust.

Psalm 147:6 NLT

Humble Yourself

Do nothing out of selfish ambition or vain conceit. Rather, in humility value others above yourselves, not looking to your own interests but each of you to the interests of the others.

Philippians 2:3-4 NIV

Haughtiness goes before destruction; humility precedes honor.

Proverbs 18:12 NLT

He guides the humble in what is right and teaches them His way.

Psalm 25:9 NIV

"He who is greatest among you shall be your servant. And whoever exalts himself will be humbled, and he who humbles himself will be exalted."

Matthew 23:11-12 NKJV

The LORD takes pleasure in His people; He adorns the humble with salvation.

Psalm 149:4 ESV

Keep a Strong Faith

Jesus said, "All things are possible
for one who believes."

Mark 9:23 ESV

We live by faith, not by sight.

2 Corinthians 5:7 NIV

"I tell you the truth, if you had faith even
as small as a mustard seed, you could say
to this mountain, 'Move from here to there,'
and it would move. Nothing would be
impossible."

Matthew 17:20 NLT

Now faith is the substance of things hoped
for, the evidence of things not seen.

Hebrews 11:1 NKJV

For in the gospel the righteousness of God
is revealed – a righteousness that is by faith
from first to last, just as it is written: "The
righteous will live by faith."

Romans 1:17 NIV

Keep a Strong Faith

What good is it if someone claims to have faith but has no deeds? Can such faith save them? Suppose a brother or a sister is without clothes and daily food. If one of you says to them, "Go in peace; keep warm and well fed," but does nothing about their physical needs, what good is it? In the same way, faith by itself, if it is not accompanied by action, is dead. But someone will say, "You have faith; I have deeds." Show me your faith without deeds, and I will show you my faith by my deeds.

James 2:14-18 NIV

Faith comes from hearing the message, and the message is heard through the word about Christ.

Romans 10:17 NIV

Without faith it is impossible to please Him, for he who comes to God must believe that He is, and that He is a rewarder of those who diligently seek Him.

Hebrews 11:6 NKJV

Keep a Strong Faith

I can do everything through Christ,
who gives me strength.

Philippians 4:13 NLT

Everyone who believes that Jesus
is the Christ has been born of God,
and everyone who loves the Father
loves whoever has been born of Him.

1 John 5:1 ESV

We know that a person is made right with
God by faith in Jesus Christ, not by obeying
the law. And we have believed in Christ
Jesus, so that we might be made right with
God because of our faith in Christ, not
because we have obeyed the law. For
no one will ever be made right with
God by obeying the law.

Galatians 2:16 NLT

"Anyone who believes and is baptized
will be saved. But anyone who refuses
to believe will be condemned."

Mark 16:16 NLT

PATIENTLY WAIT

Consider the farmers who patiently wait
for the rains in the fall and in the spring.
They eagerly look for the valuable harvest
to ripen. You, too, must be patient. Take
courage, for the coming of the Lord is near.

James 5:7-8 NLT

The LORD is good to those who wait for
Him, to the soul who seeks Him. It is
good that one should wait quietly
for the salvation of the LORD.

Lamentations 3:25-26 ESV

Wait on the LORD, and keep His way, and
He shall exalt you to inherit the land; when
the wicked are cut off, you shall see it.

Psalm 37:34 NKJV

I waited patiently for the LORD; He
inclined to me and heard my cry. He
drew me up from the pit of destruction,
out of the miry bog, and set my feet upon
a rock, making my steps secure.

Psalm 40:1-2 ESV

PATIENTLY WAIT

Wait patiently for the LORD. Be brave and courageous. Yes, wait patiently for the LORD.

Psalm 27:14 NLT

I wait for the LORD, my whole being waits, and in His word I put my hope. I wait for the Lord more than watchmen wait for the morning, more than watchmen wait for the morning.

Psalm 130:5-6 NIV

My soul, wait silently for God alone, for my expectation is from Him. He only is my rock and my salvation; He is my defense; I shall not be moved. In God is my salvation and my glory; the rock of my strength, and my refuge, is in God.

Psalm 62:5-7 NKJV

From of old no one has heard or perceived by the ear, no eye has seen a God besides You, who acts for those who wait for Him.

Isaiah 64:4 ESV

Patiently Wait

Truly my soul silently waits for God;
from Him comes my salvation.

Psalm 62:1 NKJV

Be still before the LORD and wait patiently
for Him; fret not yourself over the one who
prospers in his way, over the man who carries
out evil devices! Refrain from anger, and
forsake wrath! Fret not yourself; it tends only to
evil. For the evildoers shall be cut off, but those
who wait for the LORD shall inherit the land.

Psalm 37:7-9 ESV

Our soul waits for the LORD;
He is our help and our shield.

Psalm 33:20 NKJV

The Lord is not slow in keeping His promise,
as some understand slowness. Instead He
is patient with you, not wanting anyone to
perish, but everyone to come to repentance.

2 Peter 3:9 NIV

Practice Gentleness

Be completely humble and gentle; be patient,
bearing with one another in love.

Ephesians 4:2 NIV

You have also given me the shield of Your
salvation; Your right hand has held me up,
Your gentleness has made me great.

Psalm 18:35 NKJV

Let your gentleness be evident to all.
The Lord is near.

Philippians 4:5 NIV

Don't repay evil for evil. Don't retaliate
with insults when people insult you.
Instead, pay them back with a blessing.
That is what God has called you to do,
and He will grant you His blessing.

1 Peter 3:9 NLT

The meek shall inherit the land and delight
themselves in abundant peace.

Psalm 37:11 ESV

Practice Gentleness

Pursue righteousness and a godly life,
along with faith, love, perseverance,
and gentleness.

1 Timothy 6:11 NLT

Therefore, as God's chosen people, holy
and dearly loved, clothe yourselves with
compassion, kindness, humility, gentleness
and patience.

Colossians 3:12 NIV

"Take My yoke upon you. Let Me teach you,
because I am humble and gentle at heart,
and you will find rest for your souls."

Matthew 11:29 NLT

A servant of the Lord must not quarrel
but be gentle to all, able to teach, patient,
in humility correcting those who are in
opposition, if God perhaps will grant them
repentance, so that they may know the truth.

2 Timothy 2:24-25 NKJV

Practice Gentleness

The believers … should be obedient,
always ready to do what is good. They
must not slander anyone and must avoid
quarreling. Instead, they should be gentle
and show true humility to everyone.

Titus 3:1-2 NLT

Always be prepared to give an answer to
everyone who asks you to give the reason
for the hope that you have. But do this
with gentleness and respect, keeping a
clear conscience, so that those who speak
maliciously against your good behavior in
Christ may be ashamed of their slander.

1 Peter 3:15-16 NIV

A gentle answer deflects anger,
but harsh words make tempers flare.

Proverbs 15:1 NLT

Seek Him First

"Seek the Kingdom of God above all else,
and live righteously, and He will
give you everything you need."

Matthew 6:33 NLT

Let the hearts of those who seek the
Lord rejoice! Seek the Lord and His strength;
seek His presence continually! Remember
the wondrous works that He has done, His
miracles and the judgments He uttered.

1 Chronicles 16:10-12 ESV

I seek You with all my heart; do not
let me stray from Your commands.

Psalm 119:10 NIV

Seek the Lord your God, and you will
find Him if you seek Him with all your
heart and with all your soul.

Deuteronomy 4:29 NKJV

Seek Him First

The Lord looks down from heaven on all
mankind to see if there are any who
understand, any who seek God.

Psalm 14:2 NIV

"Ask, and it will be given to you; seek,
and you will find; knock, and it will be
opened to you. For everyone who asks
receives, and the one who seeks finds, and
to the one who knocks it will be opened."

Matthew 7:7-8 ESV

Seek the Lord while He may be found;
call upon Him while He is near; let
the wicked forsake His way, and the
unrighteous man His thoughts; let Him
return to the Lord, that He may have
compassion on him, and to our God,
for He will abundantly pardon.

Isaiah 55:6-7 ESV

"Seek the kingdom of God, and all
these things shall be added to you."

Luke 12:31 NKJV

Seek Him First

Those who seek the Lord lack no good thing.

Psalm 34:10 NIV

Let all those who seek You rejoice and be glad in You; let such as love Your salvation say continually, "The Lord be magnified!"

Psalm 40:16 NKJV

Those who know Your name put their trust in You, for You, O Lord, have not forsaken those who seek You.

Psalm 9:10 ESV

Come close to God, and God will come close to you.

James 4:8 NLT

Whatever you do, whether in word or deed, do it all in the name of the Lord Jesus.

Colossians 3:17 NIV

"Blessed rather are those who hear the word of God and obey it."

Luke 11:28 NIV

STUDY HIS WORD

All Scripture is inspired by God and is useful to teach us what is true and to make us realize what is wrong in our lives. It corrects us when we are wrong and teaches us to do what is right. God uses it to prepare and equip His people to do every good work.

2 Timothy 3:16-17 NLT

Don't just listen to God's word. You must do what it says. Otherwise, you are only fooling yourselves. For if you listen to the word and don't obey, it is like glancing at your face in a mirror. You see yourself, walk away, and forget what you look like. But if you look carefully into the perfect law that sets you free, and if you do what it says and don't forget what you heard, then God will bless you for doing it.

James 1:22-25 NLT

Jesus answered, "It is written: 'Man shall not live on bread alone, but on every word that comes from the mouth of God.'"

Matthew 4:4 NIV

STUDY HIS WORD

For the word of God is alive and active.
Sharper than any double-edged sword, it
penetrates even to dividing soul and spirit,
joints and marrow; it judges the thoughts
and attitudes of the heart.

Hebrews 4:12 NIV

"Keep this Book of the Law always
on your lips; meditate on it day
and night, so that you may be careful
to do everything written in it. Then you
will be prosperous and successful."

Joshua 1:8 NIV

"Everyone then who hears these words of
Mine and does them will be like a wise man
who built his house on the rock. The rain fell,
and the floods came, and the winds blew ...
but it did not fall. And everyone who hears
these words of Mine and does not do them
will be like a foolish man who built his house
on the sand. The rain fell, and the floods came
... and it fell, and great was the fall of it."

Matthew 7:24-27 ESV

Trust in the Lord

The LORD is good, a refuge
in times of trouble. He cares
for those who trust in Him.

Nahum 1:7 NIV

Trust in the LORD forever, for the
LORD GOD is an everlasting rock.

Isaiah 26:4 ESV

"Do not let your hearts be troubled.
You believe in God; believe also in Me."

John 14:1 NIV

Trust in Him at all times, you people;
pour out your heart before Him;
God is a refuge for us.

Psalm 62:8 NKJV

Put your trust in the LORD.

Psalm 4:5 ESV

Trust in the Lord

Some trust in chariots and
some in horses, but we trust in
the name of the Lord our God.

Psalm 20:7 NIV

If we are faithful to the end, trusting God
just as firmly as when we first believed,
we will share in all that belongs to Christ.

Hebrews 3:14 NLT

Let the morning bring me word of Your
unfailing love, for I have put my trust in
You. Show me the way I should go, for to
You I entrust my life.

Psalm 143:8 NIV

"I will rescue those who love Me. I will
protect those who trust in My name."

Psalm 91:14 NLT

TRUST IN THE LORD

Trust in the LORD with all your heart,
and lean not on your own understanding;
in all your ways acknowledge Him,
and He shall direct your paths.

Proverbs 3:5-6 NKJV

Blessed is the one who trusts in the LORD.

Psalm 40:4 NIV

The fear of man brings a snare, but whoever
trusts in the LORD shall be safe.

Proverbs 29:25 NKJV

Those who listen to instruction will prosper;
those who trust the LORD will be joyful.

Proverbs 16:20 NLT

Trust in the LORD, and do good; dwell in
the land, and feed on His faithfulness.

Psalm 37:3 NKJV

Worship Him with All Your Heart

Let us worship and bow down;
let us kneel before the Lord, our Maker!

Psalm 95:6 ESV

"For where two or three are
gathered together in My name,
I am there in the midst of them."

Matthew 18:20 NKJV

Exalt the Lord our God, and worship at His
holy mountain; for the Lord our God is holy!

Psalm 99:9 ESV

Give to the Lord the glory due His name;
bring an offering, and come before Him. Oh,
worship the Lord in the beauty of holiness!

1 Chronicles 16:29 NKJV

Since we are receiving a Kingdom that is
unshakable, let us be thankful and please God
by worshiping Him with holy fear and awe.

Hebrews 12:28 NLT

Worship Him with All Your Heart

"The hour is coming, and now is, when the true worshipers will worship the Father in spirit and truth; for the Father is seeking such to worship Him. God is Spirit, and those who worship Him must worship in spirit and truth."

John 4:23-24 NKJV

I will praise You with my whole heart; before the gods I will sing praises to You. I will worship toward Your holy temple, and praise Your name for Your loving-kindness and Your truth; for You have magnified Your word above all Your name.

Psalm 138:1-2 NKJV

Let us go to His dwelling place, let us worship at His footstool, saying, "Arise, LORD, and come to Your resting place, You and the ark of Your might."

Psalm 132:7-8 NIV

Worship Him with All Your Heart

Everything on earth will worship You;
they will sing Your praises, shouting
Your name in glorious songs. Come and
see what our God has done, what awesome
miracles He performs for people!

Psalm 66:4-5 NLT

Exalt the LORD our God; worship
at His footstool! Holy is He!

Psalm 99:5 ESV

Therefore, I urge you, brothers and sisters,
in view of God's mercy, to offer your bodies
as a living sacrifice, holy and pleasing to
God – this is your true and proper worship.

Romans 12:1 NIV

"It is written, 'You shall worship the Lord
your God, and Him only shall you serve.'"

Luke 4:8 ESV